Sealed

Ri. Lee

Sealed

Published by Meghan Riley, 2020

IBSN 978-0-578-23191-4 (Paperback)

First Edition

Ri.Lee

Part 1:

make these pages drip

Part 2:

Pieces

Sealed

Ri.Lee

Attachments:

    We always seek to hold on to everything, possess everyone, and keep them forever. Yet, we admire freedom in a soul when we see it. She became free by letting go of everything and holding on to life. The men hated her for always leaving, and people close and far envied. She was attached to nothing but the world her feet walked on and the journeys she chased. She did love, but without stages. Why do we create degrees to how much we care? There was no "I am in love with you", or "I like you but not love yet". She had no hate towards anyone... she simply loved. We all have ugly pasts and bumpy roads, but she kept her eyes forward and learned from the paths she crossed. She read books to reach parts of her brain most left untouched and thought thoughts people wouldn't even dare to question. Others happiness brought her stillness. Don't seek possession seek freedom. Enjoy the lives of the people you have met and look forward to the people you will meet on your journey. We are gifted one life on this earth, it is up to you to make it beautiful. Embrace the body you were born with, challenge the mind you've been given, and change nothing

But your perspective.

Sealed

Ri.Lee

1.

make these pages drip

Sealed

mind began to
drift off
legs and hands
felt weak,
feeling your skin
next to me

somewhere between
falling asleep
and a
dream

nails ripping down
my panties
spit on your fingers
rub my lips
    shoved it in

clenched hard
    my eyes wide open

I tell you it's   y o u r s
locking eyes
      thrusting d e e p e r
you kiss my skin
    slow & soft
but you're so   r o u g h

          make me fall in l o v e

Sealed

Somethin' about a
woman's touch
that just

makes
you moan
different.

Ri.Lee

t a s t e .

eyes
    burning through me,
watching
    my body
    thrusting into him.
dripping
    down his skin,
locking eyes-
squeezing his
fingers
    into my neck,
    pulling me close-
lips parting,
    gasping for air
spitting
    down my throat
feeling it slide
down my tongue
as I
cum

lick my lips
with whatever's left
another part
of you
    inside me

as I beg you for
breath

Sealed

I watched him
reach out his
hand

To point something
out to me,

And I lost
track of his
words

imagining those
fingers

down my throat

gagging every
breath
and every
moan

                                        if only he knew

ROSE PETALS

We paused for a moment,
and it made me realize
she was even more
beautiful naked,

her hair was thick like
a wild horse, and fell
to one side laying
against her breast.

The streetlight shined
against her skin
through the window

eyes closed, slightly
smirking & I couldn't
help but lean into her.

Nipples hardened against
her bare breasts
as I wrapped my fingers
behind her head

ripping back, feeling
her lips

both unfolding, dripping
against each other
not once
        resisting the taste

Sealed

Full Moon

Across the room
& we miss each other's
presence

I could write forever
just about the way
-you lift,
one corner
of your lip

and devour me
with those eyes.

Always thought love
    wasn't about possession
    it's about appreciation

But I want to keep you..
      All of you..
I want to breathe you,

the same air from
your lungs,
to flow through my
lips and make
my heart beat

Let me gather the pieces

        you deserve all of me.

Ri.Lee

Fossils

Dance with me
in the kitchen
step on my toes
hold me tight,
let our laughter
be the music
& your heart
be the rhythm
of the night

.

Sealed

HENNESSEY

lifts me up
bends me over the
top of the bathroom
counter, watching
him watch me
through the mirror

presses his lips
on my spine &
runs them up to
my shoulders

one hand on my breast
the other between
my legs

still engaging eyes
in the glass

shoves his hand
 down my
throat, to quiet
my moan with
a gag

eyes tearing, dripping
harder, feel my cum
drenching down
his skin

Ri.Lee

pulls the sides of
my mouth with
both hands open

pressing deeper
into my body

sinking my teeth
into his fingers

whispers in my
ear I'm HIS slut

sucking the cognac
    out of our pores

take my body
    use me
        it's yours
            i'm yours

Sealed

OVER THE LIMIT

foots to the ground
cars in 6th

winds blowing the
strands of my hair
between my lips

the houses disappear as
the street lights
run with me.

Maybe it's the feeling
of getting pulled over,
maybe it's the risk of the
surrounding cars crashing
into me..

But I feel like I'm flying
      I feel free..

Ri.Lee

Secrets

Some of us find the
true meaning
of life
when we are given
our last
breath

Sealed

Laced with Grace

Feeling the lace rub
against my skin
Not for her,
   and not for him.

Throw on the record
let the music crack,
dance in the mirror
paint my eyes with black.

Lookin' into the vanity
"I do this for you baby"
wine red lipstick, let
these fingers save me

i'm always here- waiting
      for someone

someone to never come

but I am wearing this for me baby
   curl my hair and pour a
glass to save me

flip the vinyl and pull
these stockings up
biting my lip, over fillin'
this cup

Ri.Lee

You're wasting time

You've lost time

    You've got the wrong time

You will have time

     You're on time

There is no

        t

           i

               m

                   e

If you

    can

        Grasp

                the present.

                    What is time?

Sealed

"I'll hate fuck you,

and feed you

strawberry's"

                                    Sweet & Sour

Ri.Lee

Labor Day

In Athens,
all the parks
were closed

I couldn't miss
seeing the temple
of Hephaestus

I said, "follow me,
are you down to
hop the fence?"

we had the temple to ourselves

finding ancient marble
on the path

nothing around us but trees,
jumped over the cable and
went inside

didn't care about the
cameras, just this
moment feeling alive

we stood between the
pillars, making love
as the sunset

Sealed

RAW LOVE.

"I want to hear you
    gasp for air
and choke you with it..
let me see those tears
run down your face."

let me suck you till
your sick of me,
open my mouth and
watch your cum slide
down my tongue-
and fill my throat

opened my trench coat

his hands fed my
    bare body

he always wanted more
  and I always wanted him

Ri.Lee

I saw two teenagers
kissing on the corner
of the street
in the city

They weren't moving

Just lips slowly separating
still attached by the
upper lip

And in their world no one
else was moving
as I walked past them

Is that how we used to feel?

Sealed

he said

"i'm infatuated with your scent I
        can still smell you
                on my
                        fingers........."

Ri.Lee

I
gave you
poetry books-
and you traded me
pages of philosophy.

Nothing left of you but pages

Sealed

BEING

```
young mind planning
so hard for his
future
grew old dwelling
on the past
and missed
his whole
```

```
          p
            r
              e
                s
                  e
                    n
                      c
                        e
```

equal parts.

It was like each one
of them took a part
of me

a

piece of me,

I'll never get back,

some try to put it back
together, like an old
puzzle that was never
finished,

some think I've gone mad
and keep the piece in their
pocket for a memory on a
rainy day,
but then there's that one
that fights with no armor

and tries to catch me from
running against the
                    wind

Sealed

Concentration

I read him books

while his
tongue reads

between my lips..

Ri.Lee

Some call them
dreams
but to me
it is a portal
to an alternate
reality.

Time is a myth
where just
we exist

I could feel
you there-
and
touch
your lips

All our mistakes
never happened

in this dimension

please don't wake me up

I do not want to lose
you here too

Long nights.

Sealed

You find me

lookin' up to a dark sky
in a parking lot, and come
behind me just
to point out the moon.

Ri.Lee

sometimes things get repetitive throughout
          our stories.

become conscious,

realize the thought
          behind the thought...

Sealed

AROMA

He asked me, "How
does it feel?"
couldn't recognize
any words to reveal

thoughts are unconscious,
concentrating on the surface
of his skin.

Only using our senses,
        feeling his ambience

caught up in the clocks motion,
        ingesting his dominance
fingers gripping my neck,
        unfolding my confidence

his mouth inhaling my
precipitation,
drenching his
tongue in my
foundation

biting into the sheets,
he drags me to the
 end of the bed
lifts me up by the hips
burying his head between
my legs

Ri.Lee

slams me down
into the mattress

  my hands behind me

confined to the bed
    sweet captivity.

Sealed

CHOICES

deciding between here
     and there
i want to be there
but somethings trying to
keep me here
& if I stay
here
I'll never get there

but
being
there
is
  never
    here

Ri.Lee

MUTUAL

He's curious-
watches my hands..
-teeth dig into my lips,
all he wonders is what I am
thinking about when I break the skin

In all honesty,
I didn't think he was
ready for an answer,
his interest fired in me
more and more

My movements became s l o w e r
as I felt his eyes burning
through me,
taunting him-
twirling the ends of my hair

running the tip of
my tongue
against the layers
of my lipstick.
in his mind this is
all a tease
but its always been
more than that

love has never been safe,
and I've become good at
        holding back….

Sealed

The next days

Eye to eye & were both blind,
lost in words I can't find
walking towards the door
clip the joint

mind slips back to
the breaking point

Legs get numb, tremble
against the wall
scrape my nails down
my neck, imagining it all

trying to fight it but my
insides scramble
eyes roll behind my head
squeezing on to the door
handle

couple hours later
sitting at my desk,
I see your reflection in
the window glass

my hearts off beat
squeezing into the seat

feel you in my bones
from across the room

Ri.Lee

let the scent of my
desires
burn through your nose
like a perfume..

Sealed

I see you in
everyone's face

their dark brown eyes
turn into your eyes

their hands turn into your hands...

But not their lips.

I can still close my eyes
and taste the memories of
time
freezing the instant the
creases of your lips touched
mine

I always run from the rain.

Ri.Lee

We barely said a
word yet out
skin spoke for us

Wondering if you
could feel my heart
pounding through my
chest

Could you read my thoughts
by the exchanging between
our hands

You wrap your arm
around my neck
squeezing our shells
together

Kiss turns into a bite
and I don't want to let
you go

don't say goodbye

                    I want to replay these moments

Sealed

Time.Don't.Wake.Us.

Let's make a song
with the sun
watching us through
the blinds

Nothing left of our
souls but
broken pieces for us
to find.

Record spinning
simultaneously with
the pace of our hearts

Lift me up against
the dresser
as out lips fall
together and
fall
   apart

Ri.Lee

You laughed when
I told you I still
read your letters

but when the world feels fake

and love is unattained

I find something real in your words.

Sealed

MALAGA

Sitting in the sand
in the opposite direction,
stared at the back of
his head looking for a reaction.

Sand in the creases
of my bare skin
sun beaming on my breasts
mind at ease with the wind

Malaga, La Playa
close my eyes
feel the waves
crash into me
heard a soft voice in
the distance say
"Isn't this the most
beautiful thing?"

looked over she smiled,
where did she come from?
she was fucking the waves
making love with the sun

thrusting herself against
the current
she was from Switz
brown hair fell to the
edges of her hips

ocean split her
top in the middle
my insides clenched,
the cold water laid
against her skin
but she was still
quenched

Sealed

Typewriter

I'd fuck
these keys
with the chills from
your memories

at the light of Fredrick
and Passaic
closed my eyes in
the middle of the day

run my hands up my neck
let these chills chase
my skin
flashbacks to last night
every inch your lips been

my chest tightens

the light turns green,
my fingers on the outer
    lace of my panties
dripping at the scene

pressing on the gas
squeezing my fingers
between my lips,
one hand on the wheel
while the others

catching drips

take my hand from under
my dress
suck these fingers
dry,
biting at the edge of
my finger
pulling the car over
to the side

cars in park, sun shining
through the window
while I light a menthol,
watch these ashes fall
cum dripping on the rental

Sealed

He painted to mirror his visions

she had to convince imaginations to build
their own world

off her words.

P I C A S S O

stroked the tip
of his brush
on my inner thigh,
painting images
in my head
of him deep
inside

presses his chest
against my
breasts, licks
my ear down to
my neck

squirts the
paint onto the
canvas,
squeezes the tube
no drops
left

bottom cheeks on
the white surface,
undoes himself and
enters my legs,
wrapping them around
his body-
a masterpiece only

Sealed

we interpret

dipping our fingers
into the pallets as
we massaged each other's
skin

rhythm of our shells
to create the composition

slide my blue down
his face, so he knows
where to paint…
red on his hands imprint
on my neck,

slamming me down into
the canvas

ran his mouth up my
stems as he painted
my petals,
blossoming in seconds-
a taste he will always
remember

mounting on top of me,
colors combining
almost rolling to the edge,
we pause, he shoves
his brush
        inside me

lips locked hips locked
grinding as the colors flow
I become the focal point
when his eyes can't
let go

thrusted him into the
foreground, conquering
his textures

poured the tin of purple
down my shoulders
mixing within the
yellows

warm colors
slide down the margins
of my nipples
blending the reds of
his hands, painting
my breasts as they
dribble

forcing my hips
against his pelvis,
repetition of our
bodies just
flow with it-
souls are infused,
rubs my clit with
his hues

Sealed

clutching on to
my breasts as our
colors splash,
moaning his name to
the sky, with my
last breath

left his signature
on me
as I dripped down
to his chest

we looked back at
our collaboration-

nothing but the contours of
me   and   him

an abstract masterpiece-

made with love

by our imprints.

when love dripped from his lips

"we miss each other even when we're right in front
of our faces..."

Sealed

CAPTURED MY EYE

I walked into the water
only saw her face,
her eyes lit up in
the reflection of the
lake

combination of yellows
and greens,
wanted to swim inside
her, but I couldn't
intervene

she was flowing with
the waves of the water,
as she began to walk out

drops off her body slowly
fall into my mouth

her body was perfected
by the gods,
they sat at a table and
perfected all the odds

one foot in front of
the other while her slim
hips shook her curves
up and down

Ri.Lee

I begged her with my
eyes as I fell to the
ground

she paid no mind to me
as she laid at the edge
of the lake,
breasts slightly fell to
the side
gradually diving her legs

pressed my lips against
her lips
barely licking the seam

taunting her soul
back of her knees twitch
tease with the tip
of my tongue
maker her beg for it

no hesitate,

she couldn't wait-

thrusting herself up
against my face

watching her jaw
slowly descend as
she feels my fingers
penetrate

Sealed

vulnerable to my hands
dripping over and
over again

pushed her down,
jam my fingers deep
against her tongue

sucks them dry
each
  and every
      drop
        of cum.

Ri.Lee

XCHANGING FANTASIES

it rained outside and
in my sleep,
we met at the park
right by the police

a little over by
the swings
we walked past the
cameras smiling

it was dark-
rain pouring from
the stars
soakin' wet in the
middle of the park

drops sliding down
my skin,
dry me with your lips-
running into the
playground
follow me to the bridge

stepping up the
ladder, feel your
hands up my dress,
tips of your fingers
notice there's nothing
underneath

Sealed

pull my dress up slowly
so you crave
what you'll
eat

crawling down the boarders
of the bridge,
chest is on fire-
anticipating you
within

pin me down,
    squeeze my wrists
press your body
inside

moaning in your
ear as your biting
on mine

intertwining our
legs, no space
in between

hitting into that
spot over
and over,
fighting to hold
my words in

when our lips
get stuck

and our eyes
both close

the beating
of our chests
becomes the
only
sound
in the
world.

Sealed

cases of beer
capsules of all colors
we met at the corner
walked in with a crowd
sneakin' grabs
so no one saw us

girls on the couch
talkin' bout
the way your lips look
so seductive the way
you part your mouth

& the boys to your left
tryna look up my dress
and we're in the middle
of this trying to repress

lifted up his solo cup
smirkin' at me
inhalin' my cig
slowly
just to chill out
the speed

throw down my school I.D
emptied out the script
took a couple bumps
told him I had the rest
in the car

he followed me out
didn't make it
down the steps
back against the
neighbor's door
face between my legs

goose bumps ran down
my inner thigh
feelin' just the tip
of his tongue inside
looks up at me devouring
me alive

people walkin' up to
to the front door
tryna party
we're running down
the steps lookin' for
somewhere to hide me

laundry room to the
apartments, sits me
up on the washer
leaned forward barely
a kiss, and I'm dripping
like a faucet

machine wasn't on and
we rocked that metal,
chipping paint off
the walls

Sealed

he wasn't the type
to speak
his eyes ate at me
while my moan
peaked

felt me soakin' his
legs, all down
his shaft
biting into my lips
can't even let out a
gasp

put his finger in
my mouth
slowly sucked it
out
vibrated with his
skin
placed his hands on
my hips
closing our eyes
feeling the world
between our
lips.

Ri.Lee

HOURGLASS

peel me to
the core
I want you to
ignore
the outer
layers of
my brain
and skip right
through the pain

and look for me
underneath

I swear you'll find
a piece

of you,

that your soul
hasn't found
it's just us on
the ground

the worlds spinning
beneath us
and were trembling
with reasons

destroying us before
we've even tried

Sealed

I swear I've seen the
world in the
pupils of your eyes

friction of our skin
imprisons my mind

and I'll sit here and
wait until we both
realize we're running
out of time...

Ri.Lee

DON'T THINK

laid on his lap
lookin' up through
the branches
of the trees
malboro reds in my
hand
cold 40oz between my
knees
eye to eye and were glued
talkin' bout all the
books we've been through

places
we've both seen
and how this is where
we're meant to
be

the worlds spinning
and were sitting
in place
nothing to do-
we spent the day
on the bench
scenic view of the
hood, but our bodies
are drenched

in our minds clashing

Sealed

words people keep to
themselves
the sun is watching us
on the mountain top

we look for rain
on these sunny
days
overweighing
the risk of us
breaking away

Ri.Lee

looking down
at my legs
around the sides
of her head

knees on
her chest
squeezing my
hands

around her neck

feeling her try to
gasp for air
with my cum
on her lips

take all of it.

Sealed

Legs intertwined
feet rubbing together
hips align with
your hips
arms wrapped through
each other

your heart beating
against my back
and mine
in your hands

mouth breathing on
the back of my neck
my hair in your face
just pieced
together

puzzle pieces.

Ri.Lee

Split my hair
into two
wrapped the strands
around his thick hands

pulling my head
back against the center
of my
shoulder blades

ends of my hair

fell against my cheeks

as he pulled harder
whispering in my ear

"have you been a

        bad girl…?"

Sealed

this time was different.

Thanksgiving-
leaned me down
held my body
up into yours

squeezed me into
your skin
feeling each time
your lips
leave imprints

up my neck
as you thrust
slow

my eyes
closed

is this what it
feels like to
make love?

each touch of your
hands intensify
leaving my heart
 e x p o s e d.

Ri.Lee

He loved when I
couldn't breathe-
pressed my head
deeper

looking down at me

locking eyes, saliva
dripping out of the
edges of my lips

tears running down
my face

just when he knew
there wasn't much
more I could
take

puts both
hands around my neck,
    choking me

if only you could feel
how soaked my panties are

                you're mine to please.

71

Sealed

Rain drops-

hitting the windshield

seatbelt wrapped

    around his

        neck

vulnerable,   anticipating

 my   t o u c h

i'm in control

feel your blood rushhhhhh

Ri.Lee

GWB

Broadway plays,
and Hennessey
bottles
in our pockets

driving over
the bridge

hitting the
highest
RpM

hop over the
seat, on to
your lap

leg ramming
into the door
moonlight shining
through the
window

put the window
down a little,
my hairs in your
face as you're trying
to drive

we both let out

Sealed

```
a light moan
you can barely
hear over the exhaust

riding into
your body, don't let
your eyes get
lost

kissing on your
neck as you
down shift

skyline of the
city watching
us drift.
```

Ri.Lee

Took his hand out
from between
my legs

and our lips met
against his fingers

locking eyes

both tasting me

let me taste you..

Sealed

Ri.Lee

2.

      P

        I

          E

            C

              E

                S

…..

Sealed

Ri.Lee

After they've peeled
our petals,
and watched us
stand in the sun

trying not to wilt

they walked away
without even seeing
if we were drying out

but we stood tall

all of us

still hopeful deep down
that someday,
someone,
will stand in the sun
with us.

for years we've given
our petals away,
and still we stay
we stand
we wait

even with them taking
bits and pieces from us,
we face our left over
dis colored

Sealed

petals out into the wind

we have hope

     we had hope

but we never needed you.

We have each other.

Ri.Lee

How do I tell
you I'm scared?

of losing parts
of me again

I'm broken into
pieces

& I don't have
any of me
to lend.

Sealed

Don't be so modest

People like to say they live their life
with no regrets and never look back.
Each life we live is based off a previous
choice. Except each choice is played out
in ten different scenarios. Once you role
with the script, you can never say cut and
go back. When I am alone and everything
becomes still, I try to imagine where we
would be if I stayed.

Ri.Lee

It's hard
to say
I love you
when someone
took advantage
of those words

it's hard for me to
feel I can trust you
when someone never
let me in

it's hard for me to
do things for you
when someone had
selfish intentions

it's hard for me to
feel enough for you
when so many parts of
me have been
broken.

Sealed

STILLNESS.

Sitting in the windowsill
smell of fresh cut grass
all the plants are standing still
yet I slip into the past

we never spoke like others
of people and each other
just the world and our dreams
and how we fit in between

on your porch we promised
to meet
not more not less than
once a week
now I'm miles across the sea

if I walked past you on the street
we would be fighting eye contact

strangers in a crowd

walking past

Ri.Lee

This isn't me
and it is hard
to explain why

I don't show you
too much love
sometimes
because so much
of me, has been
taken from
me

I wasn't able to
express myself
for so long, so
now when I don't get
my way I get mad
easily

To someone, I
wasn't good enough
for years, so when
you need time to get
to know me

I do not have it

Don't know the difference
of someone taking
advantage of me, or
that really cares

Sealed

so I react differently
every time
you're there

it's not a wall
I built up
i'm trying to
not give a
fuck

when deep down
inside all I am
is

craving your love.

Ri.Lee

Put yourself in my shoes, I'm not the one for you.

Opposite corners and you
watch her
gliding, dress
flowing

she picks up her glass of
wine, and the imprints
of her lipstick on the
rim of the glass

weakens your devils

crushed your ribs

she's yours but you can't
look away
most women's flaws
turn you, but hers
you display

walls collapsing every time
her heels hit the floor

dodging bricks to follow her
through whatever is left of
the door

you're the shadow of her smile

Sealed

when she speaks you're choking
on her eyes

someone calls her name
in the distance,
those six letters
make your chest cry

caught up in the morning hours
placing the pieces of
her hair resting on her
jawline
behind her ear,

watching her sleep, so
she won't disappear

I hope you find someone
who makes you
  feel again
makes you complete

love can be a blessing,
but for the cold
it's defeat

Ri.Lee

I read your love
letters to go
back in time
it makes the story
feel real again.

You know the ones
where two people fall
in love and never
speak again?

then your words make it
all real.

The first time you
Said "I love you"

the way you smelled
comes off the paper

the nights we stayed up
laughing and talking
about the universe
out on the grass

all comes back.

Sealed

Monsters

The problem is I fell
in love with a part
of him that comes
and goes
like a
flicking lightbulb

When it's dark I can't
help but look for
the light
in you
to
save me.

FLASHFORWARDS

I imagine you years from now

with someone you deserve…

your kids sleeping between

you both

and the moonlight shining

against the creases of her face

and you're still awake…

i'm suckin' on whisky

ice cubes at a bar in

San Jose

and I can't help but

think

if leaving was a

mistake

Sealed

I hope you didn't burn the letters

and you read them to keep

us alive

there are still blurred words

with tear drops on the

one you wrote me when

we were kids

Are you keeping us alive?

Ri.Lee

Sometimes I wonder

My clone would have married you
and had tons of babies that
looked just like you
& we would stay up late together
after the kids fell asleep,
drink cheap whisky while we
looked up at the sky and
talked about our day

No matter where we lived
I wouldn't care because I
would be with you,
happy

I would've made you
breakfast

reminded you of everything
you had to do
surprise you with little
gifts and notes

But I'm not a clone
I'm me
and my decisions have
let me be
free.

Sealed

Give her the sun

and she will grow

Give her the moon

and she will awake

filled with color

Give her nothing

and she will be

born again

without you.

Ri.Lee

I did you a favor by
not coming back

You don't want to love a mess like this

Sealed

The sun through the blinds
as we danced in the living
room with no music

moments like this is what I missed

I cried behind my sunglasses
as you pulled me close

running out the door
without saying
g o o d b y e

I can no longer try...

Ri.Lee

This used to
be like our place
with the views
of the lake

I'd write in
the corner
and you would
sketch in your
space

Two artists in love

walkin' down the streets
of antiques
sunsets here are
so bittersweet

now that I'm standing
alone on the lake

where we used to be.

Sealed

you used to tell me
not to say

I
Love
You

So much

And now as I walk away
    You seem to have found the words

                         So much...

Ri.Lee

hands around my neck
squeezing out my last breath

words thrown at me that
would take you a few steps
closer to death

spent nights staring at
the phone for a call

sat by the window waiting
for someone to come home

drank & popped pills so
I could sleep through the
tears

fed so many lies, I lied to
myself to get through the
years

found messages from women
that were more than
just friends

made myself feel not enough
just to make amends

                              not anymore.

Sealed

2AM

Reading poetry
under the covers,
hoping each car
I hear turn the corner
was your car

I would pause and
listen for the
rumbles of your
exhaust…

as I wait for
hours for you
to show up
I'm still waiting
years for you to
love me .

Ri.Lee

Fossils

I fell into your eyes at a gas station, as we waited
for our milkshakes. You were instant air through my
    lungs pulling me out of the water. I could look
    back at that day and remember every detail… it's
    recorded in my brain and I love to press play. My
    turquoise and grey floral summer dress, long blonde
    curls pulled up in a ponytail. Your dread locks
past your shoulders, and eyes disappearing with your
    smile. I felt like I could make you fall in love
with me the way I just did with you. You mentioned
the word destiny once, how we both chose that time,
and that place. I found you-you found me. But once
you had me, I was never worthy to be yours. Jumping
 in the air for a fresh start, I was waving my arms
 for you to SEE me. When I fell in love the first
    day backing up against the door on my way out, we
both smiled with our eyes and our face. You asked
me for my name and forgot it on the way out. You
    told me yours and I still can't get it out of my
                         head…

Sealed

Squeeze on to shells when I sleep,
pulse in my ear but I don't feel
a heart beat

counting the sheep

tripping over fences as the
night hunts the weak

and I look to the ceiling

not the sky or the moon but
the cracks in the beam

squeeze on to his torso just
to find a beat

eat my food cold so I can
feel something

I found out about the leaves

why they change colors and run
from the trees

curl up on the ground and
watch the others spring

but you don't fool me.

Ri.Lee

Don't lose the pieces

"how could I be wrong?" I thought...

I opened up the same door
he shattered

forgive me heart, for yet
I have been forsaken

How dare
I give
a
piece of
you
away
without asking.

Sealed

I tasted you,
in a sip of green tea.
I found your art
in the walls of
graffiti

I feel your warmth
somewhere left
in my cold
lonely sheets

running my hands
across them
as I try to
fall asleep

I look for
you in the roads
missing our
sceneries

I try to see beauty
in what I used to
love about pink skies,
somethings missing
in the passenger
seat when I drive

I look for you in
the cobblestone streets

of the city

time has eaten away at
the words
do You Miss Me.

You are everywhere.

and nowhere.

Sealed

INNER SAVIOR

I went back for
you
in that house

the lights were off
and you were lying
somewhere in
between the
faucet drops

sun wasn't resting
between the blinds
and your soul
hasn't returned to
you in years.

Felt your ego
inside me

watched you stroke
with your eyes closed

My soul fought to
find yours, but the
pieces left were
decomposed.

Unapologetic.

Sealed

Nightmares or
call it dreams,
I keep running into
you and not being
able to breathe

I bump into you
at a store, and I
fall to the floor

cover my face
and just cry and cry

it wasn't like bumping
into a stranger I used
to love...

it was like finding
someone I love that
died...

Ri.Lee

And in time
you get to a point
of clarity.
it could take months
or maybe years, but
you'll get there
I promise

the pain settles
in your heart for
a moment

and your mind
reminds you of the nights
you didn't sleep

all the times you cried

the women on the side

all the worrying
is gone
the lies & mistrust

you'll find yourself at
      peace
and all your
      pieces
         adjust.

Sealed

I gave you
half of me,
maybe a little
more than half.

and I don't
want it back.

I want you to
carry it with you.
sleep with it,
eat with it,
lay with your women
with it,

And feel me every day of your life.

Somedays I
visit all the
little places we would
stop at.

the bank across
the field

the Walgreens we would
look for toy cars

the view of the city
by the skatepark

at the red light,
I look through the
diner window

maybe we're still
sitting in there

eating Belgian
chocolate chip waffles
and
chicken wings.

Sealed

I let too
much time
go by

I lost myself
and I lost
You.

Ri.Lee

The new car
is a hole

solo flights
were just a hole

numbness on the
drive to work,
the sitting on
the shower floor

looking out the
small airplane
window holding
back tears,
the waiting for
the months to
stop passing

the music that doesn't
comfort,
you feel it.

the people you see
are just a hole

the impulsive plans
and ideas
are just a hole

Sealed

```
the books to
escape to are
just
a
hole

that I can
no longer
fill
with
you.
```

Ri.Lee

I took a sip of
the hot green tea
and immediately

flashed back to
you and me

in between

the mountains and
temples of Japan

all in one sip

I met you
in an old place
where we drank

in love.

will you ever not be
in every object
I touch?

Sealed

Everything I do
is a distraction
from you

when the clocks pause

and no ones in the room

I somehow enjoy to cry

Because I can finally

Feel. You.

Ri.Lee

Driving slow
riding the waves
trying to stay
between the dotted
lines

I'm hypnotized

looking for your
face in the corner
of my eyes

like we used to ride.

Sealed

I miss our
hot tea
winter nights
and
watermelon
summers.

The mountainous
horizon surrounding
Bogota,
getting lost in
the rain forest of
Costa Rica

The beer you'll drink
in Dublin,
All the places in Paris
that will give you
flashbacks of us

Vineyards in Italy-
where we made
love

you couldn't forget
me
in the tallest building
of Malaysia

You're running
to forget me
but I'm all
you'll ever
think of.

Sealed

We always

chased the sun
with the rain
in the rear view
mirror
and the music
in another language
playing in the background
while we drove
through the alps,
through the deserts,
along the seas

just you & me.

Ri.Lee

The smallest thing
as cookin'
eggs in the morning
and remembering
you showing me
that it is easier
if you crack
hard boiled
eggs from the
bottom-
peeling them open,
and were sitting
on the kitchen
counters
laughing,
eating together

just brought me back
to where I tried
to hide
you in my brain

I just can't erase you

Sealed

These nights.

Ruffle sleeve cropped top
off the shoulders,
pleated flowing white skirt
dancing salsa in the center
of the crowd

your silky black curls
in my face
as our bodies
filled the space

hips coinciding in motion

our hands up in
the air
pressed together

running the tips of our
fingers down each others
body, swaying closely,
music beating
faster and slower

lights flashing different
colors against
our skin

Ri.Lee

spinning me around, press
my body into yours
turn over my shoulder
our lips
meet
as we
dance.

Sealed

TWO.

One of you has
a beautiful smile.
and eyes that would
disappear as soon
as you laughed

ready to explore
your curiosities
of the world.

Mannerisms-
weird expressions
and unexplainable
things we would do
they made no sense,
but we knew.

Love, that people
would see as soon as
we would meet.

how we met,

you used to say
destiny,
 somethin'
like we were meant
to be

one of you has insecurities,
that left you not trusting anyone,
not even me

one of you has a part of you
that doesn't want to be loved
or seen

so you don't get hurt

one of you says things that
would break my heart
over and over
again.

One of you wants things
your way, any other way
you don't understand

and you can't put
yourself in other people's
 shoes

one of you wants to be alone,
yet scared to lose

one of you will never see
what. went. wrong.

Sealed

when you love, you
have to
love

you can't wait until
it's gone.

Ri.Lee

Our heads out the
window, backs against
the bed

staring up at the
sky watching the
eclipse

blowing smoke
up into the night
while we watched
the moon disappear

felt like nothing
existed
in the world

just. us.   here.

Sealed

Made the mistake
of loving you
more than
I loved
myself

that is when
vulnerability
ate me
till there was
nothing. left.

Ri.Lee

I can't feel anything.

This music,
the morning
drive to work

the sun hitting
my skin
when I walk
out the door,

the few drinks
at the bar
the few that turns
into more.

I'm numb without you.

Sealed

After

you couldn't
possibly
know how it felt

walking out of
your house in the
pouring rain.
my heels in my hand,
the mascara
running down
my face

my bare feet
walking
through the
puddles of dirt
down the concrete
sidewalks

feeling
nothing
and
everything
at once

                              what you did.

Ri.Lee

Music faded
behind me,
the drinks
turned into
nothing
but empty
glasses of
ice

and somehow
I see your
face in
the trance
of the
lights

                                    Heartbreak

Sealed

We would go to the theater
every week, but this
time was different

I was waiting outside
in a pink floral
skirt with black
stiletto heels

long lace kimono that
fringed down to my
knees

divine wine
red lipstick
and I waited by the
door

listening for you
car to pull up
walking in circles
as I see you in the
corner

trying to hide
behind a sign

and your eyes lit up
as if they were smirking
at me the same time as

Ri.Lee

your mouth

I hid behind the
car in front of me,
we're both peaking
through the windows

I slide behind a tree,
you go two cars in front

I go to another car, you
find another sign

we meet in the middle of
the parking lot
laughing we
found
each other.
between the signs.
again.

Sealed

What if I see you
again?

in person, not just
in my dreams

I think all the weight
would shift to
my heart

and I wouldn't be
able to breathe

all the pain would
be there
        and not
            there

because I would never not

love you.

Ri.Lee

BARE.

You didn't have
to try
and I didn't
have to hide

it was our bare
selves alone
in the night

you on
the toilet while
i'm in the shower

sitting on the
bathroom
floor telling
stories

sipping tea
in the winter
smoking joints
under the covers

not being able
to sleep without
each other

Sealed

we were bare.

not who we were out there.

it was a part of us no one would
ever see
or ever
know

but we knew existed

our naked souls encrypted
into pieces of each other.

A forever lover.

Ri.Lee

www.ingramcontent.com/pod-product-compliance
Lightning Source LLC
Chambersburg PA
CBHW021010090426
42738CB00007B/740